The
Wild Outdoors

GO WHITETAIL DEER HUNTING!

by Lisa M. Bolt Simons

Captivate is published by Capstone Press, an imprint of Capstone.
1710 Roe Crest Drive, North Mankato, Minnesota 56003
www.capstonepub.com

Library of Congress Cataloging-in-Publication Data
Names: Simons, Lisa M. B., 1969- author.
Title: Go whitetail deer hunting! / by Lisa M. Bolt Simons.
Description: North Mankato, Minnesota : Capstone Press, [2022] |
Series: The wild outdoors | Includes bibliographical references
and index. | Audience: Ages 8-11 | Audience: Grades 4-6 |
Summary: "Sitting in a tree, a hunter quietly scopes out the
woods. Suddenly a white tail appears. The hunter has one
chance to take the shot! Readers can join in the excitement
of whitetail deer hunting and learn everything they need to
safely enjoy the sport"— Provided by publisher.
Identifiers: LCCN 2021008432 (print) | LCCN 2021008433 (ebook) |
ISBN 9781663906151 (hardcover) | ISBN 9781663920850 (paperback) |
ISBN 9781663906120 (pdf) | ISBN 9781663906144 (kindle edition)
Subjects: LCSH: White-tailed deer hunting—Juvenile literature.
Classification: LCC SK301 .S56 2022 (print) | LCC SK301 (ebook) |
DDC 799.2/7652—dc23
LC record available at https://lccn.loc.gov/2021008432
LC ebook record available at https://lccn.loc.gov/2021008433

Image Credits
Alamy: Tiago Zegur, 12, 21; Capstone Studio: Karon Dubke, 11, 15,
16, 17, 22, 23; Getty Images: Mitch Kezar/Design Pics, 1; Newscom:
Kenneth Whitten, 27, Mitch Kezar, 19, ZUMA Press/Mitch Kezar, 13;
Science Source: Jim W. Grace, 28; Shutterstock: Amy Lutz, 7, Emily
Gust, 8, Kyle T Perry, 25, Paul Tessier, Cover, Ron Rowan Photography,
9, stockcreations, 6, Tom Reichner, 5, Zheltyshev, 24

Editorial Credits
Editor: Mandy Robbins; Designer: Jennifer Bergstrom; Media
Researcher: Jo Miller; Production Specialist: Tori Abraham

Table of Contents

Words in **bold** are in the glossary.

WHITETAIL DEER HUNTING ADVENTURE

The sun is just peeking over the horizon. The sky grows light as you watch it from your deer stand. You sit quietly, as still as you can. If you move, you may frighten the deer you've come to hunt.

You are wearing **camouflage** and blaze orange clothing. You have warm layers on in the cool autumn air. Your gun is ready. You wait for a deer to walk into view.

Your heart races when a big buck steps out from behind a tree. He heads toward a meadow. You're facing his side, which is perfect to take a shot. You don't want to move too quickly, so you wait until he's in your **range**. Then you raise your gun slowly to take your shot!

Deer meat is called venison.

Whitetail deer hunting is more than just taking down an animal. Hunting develops character. You learn self-control, patience, and responsibility. If you do get a deer, you can have fresh, lean meat to eat.

Deer hunting is also about respecting wildlife and nature. Hunting whitetail deer helps with **conservation**. It also helps control the deer population. With too many deer, the **ecosystem** is out of balance. The deer can actually hurt the land because they eat too many plants.

Deer hunters help the economy too. Money from license and tag fees, taxes, and donations is used by conservation organizations. The organizations manage the wildlife and make sure animals don't decrease in number. In the past, too much hunting almost led to some animals' **extinction**.

Before you go hunting, you have to make a plan. Today, technology can play an important role. Trail cameras, or trail cams, can be a fun way to track deer. You can set them up in the woods. Connect them to computers and smart phones to see photos and video of the animals in the area. The footage can give you hints about where the deer are and when they go there. These cameras aren't legal everywhere. Make sure you check the laws where you hunt.

A hunter checks her trail cam.

Whitetail deer leave tracks where they have been.

You don't need a trail cam to plan your hunt. You can scout the area by following tracks, trails, or tree bark rubbings. You can figure out where you want a deer stand or **blind**. You might even set up a camp. Go with an adult and shop for supplies and gear.

FACT

The whitetail deer got its name from the white fur under its tail. You can see the full white part when the deer feels scared and runs off.

Chapter 1

GEAR CHECKLIST

Gear up to make the best of your deer hunting experience. Deer hunters usually use a rifle, shotgun, or bow. Occasionally, hunters use a muzzleloader, a gun loaded through the end of the barrel. You'll also need **ammunition** or arrows.

The clothes you wear when you hunt are very important. When deer hunting using a gun, you should wear blaze orange to make sure other hunters can see you. Wear the right clothes for the weather in your area too. If you live where it's cold, wear a warm jacket, a hat, and gloves. You may want to take foot warmers and hand warmers too. If you live where it's warm, wear layers or ultralight clothing. No matter where you hunt, wear comfortable boots.

Blaze orange clothing is an important part of a deer hunter's gear.

Other gear is a must on a hunting trip. You need to have your license from the government allowing you to hunt. A deer stand or blind is important too, to help you blend in with the environment. If you plan an all-day outing, bring food such as sandwiches or granola bars. Don't take food that is loud to eat, such as chips or apples. Make sure to take juice or water, especially if the weather is hot.

A hunter looks through his scope.

Additional gear is optional. Binoculars and gun **scopes** can help hunters spot deer from a distance. Some deer hunters like to use **decoys**. Hunters can also use deer calls. Since whitetail deer have an excellent sense of smell, many hunters use scent kill. It can be sprayed on clothes and gear to cover up your scent.

A hunter places a deer decoy.

The Biggest Buck to Beat

The average buck weighs 180 pounds (82 kilograms). How much would a buck need to weigh to make it the biggest? In 1955, Horace R. Hinckley killed a buck in Maine that weighed 451 pounds (205 kg). In 1926, Carl Lenander, Jr., killed a buck in Minnesota that weighed 511 pounds (232 kg). But in 1977, John Annett killed a buck in Canada that weighed more than 540 pounds (245 kg)!

Chapter 2

RULES AND RESPONSIBILITIES

Before you go whitetail deer hunting, know the rules. A license allows you to hunt. A permit may be needed in some states for the deer **species** you plan to hunt. You need to check when you can hunt too. There are different seasons for doe and buck hunting. There are also different seasons for the kind of weapon you use.

Other responsibilities include taking classes. Hunter education courses are required in most states. If you use a gun, you must take a firearms safety course.

Before the hunting season, get plenty of shooting practice. Doing this will help with accuracy and confidence, especially when the target is a live whitetail deer.

A bowhunter takes target practice.

FACT

Antlers on adult males start to grow in the spring. The antlers grow about 0.25 inch (0.6 cm), or the size of a pinky fingernail, every day!

But where can you hunt? Public land options include national and state properties, as well as local wildlife areas. If you want to hunt on private land, ask permission from the owner. No matter where you go, be considerate and pick up after yourself when you're done for the day. Don't leave any litter behind.

Once on the property, some hunters use techniques to draw the deer closer. They may use deer calls or grunts. Some hunters rattle antlers together. Others use deer urine, or pee, to draw deer closer. Deer are attracted by the scent of other deer.

A hunter rattles antlers together to attract deer.

**A hunter applies bottled deer scent to a
branch to attract deer.**

When it's time to shoot the deer, keep the rules in
mind. Only shoot bucks during buck season and does
during doe season. Also, some states don't allow you
to kill very large deer. Make sure you're shooting with
the correct weapon for the season too.

When a deer comes into sight, it's time to take action. When you aim, make sure the deer's body is broadside. This means the deer's side is toward you. Then you can shoot at its chest behind the front leg. The deer's heart and lungs are located there. Hitting this area gives you a better chance of a clean shot. It will most likely kill the deer quickly.

"Scents" You Asked

Deer communicate in many ways. They make sounds. When they lift their tails or tuck them down, it means different things. Deer also communicate with scent. They have scent glands in their feet! Scents can help mates find each other or identify family members. Scents can also mark trails.

A hunter tracks down his kill.

After you shoot, wait 15 to 30 minutes. Then track the deer. After you find it, immediately attach the required tag to the buck's antler or doe's ear. The final step is to clean, or **dress**, the deer. Let an adult use a knife to take out the organs and drain the blood from the animal.

Chapter 3

SAFETY 101

To have a successful hunt, it's important to stay safe. Handling your weapon is one thing you learn when you complete gun and hunter safety courses.

There are many things to keep in mind when using a firearm. If you're unsure, always assume the weapon is loaded. Never climb into a tree, deer stand, or blind with a loaded gun. Always point the gun in a safe direction, and know where other hunters are around you. Keep the safety on. This part on the gun stops it from shooting. Don't put your finger on the trigger until you're ready to shoot. Make sure you know what you're shooting. Also, know what's beyond what you're shooting in case you miss and hit what's behind it.

Deer can make several hundred vocalizations. They use sounds such as grunts, bleats, and snorts to "talk" to each other.

A young bowhunter aims his weapon.

If you're bowhunting, there are some safety tips too. Only place an arrow in the string if you're ready to shoot. Always be ready to get into your shooting stance. Then you'll be able to shoot your bow at any given moment. Only point the arrow in a safe direction, making sure you know where other hunters are located.

No matter which weapon you choose, there are safety rules for deer stands. Wear a safety harness. Never hurry when you're climbing up or down. Use a haul line or rope to raise or lower your gear instead of carrying it while climbing. If you haul up a gun, make sure it's unloaded and pointing down. Do not fall asleep in a deer stand, or you could fall.

A hunter pulls her weapon up to her deer stand with a rope.

Supplies to keep you safe and help you find your way can be lifesavers when you're hunting.

When going on a hunt, it's always a good idea to plan for emergencies. Let other people know where the hunting party is going and when you'll be returning. In case you have any problems, they'll know where to find you. Take some extra items with you in case you get lost or injured. These items may include a Global Positioning System (GPS) or compass, a cell phone, a whistle, a flashlight, and a first aid kit.

Finally, you should go hunting with a responsible adult. The adult may or may not need a hunting license. Check the laws where you live. This is a good time to learn more about whitetail deer hunting and connect to the outdoors together.

Deer hunting can be a fun bonding activity for hunters.

Chapter 4

WHERE AND WHEN TO HUNT WHITETAIL DEER

The majority of whitetail deer live in the United States. They can be found in almost every state, except in the southwest. The United States has a lot of public land on which to hunt whitetail deer.

Whitetail deer also live in other places around the world. They can be found in southern Canada. In South America, they live as far south as Bolivia. You can also find whitetail deer on the other side of the ocean. They were actually taken there in the mid-1800s. Whitetail deer were released into the Czech Republic and Finland. In order to hunt in Europe, hunters must join associations. Only members can hunt. North American visitors can only hunt in Europe with tour companies, however.

Whitetail deer are protected from hunters in certain areas.

A proud young hunter poses with her kill.

Once you know where to hunt, you need to know when. Most seasons open in September or October. South Carolina is an exception. Its bowhunting season opens in August. Since every location is slightly different, make sure you check your area's hunting agencies. A state's Department of Natural Resources (DNR) is a good place to start. This organization will tell you season dates, which weapon can be used, and which deer can be hunted.

Hunting for whitetail deer can develop into a lifelong hobby. It develops skill and builds character. It teaches hunters about wildlife, how to provide meat for a family, and how to hunt safely. It may be the perfect sport for you!

GLOSSARY

ammunition (am-yuh-NI-shuhn)—bullets and other objects that can be fired from weapons

blind (BLYND)—a shelter used to protect a hunter from the weather and being seen by animals

camouflage (KA-muh-flahzh)—coloring or covering that makes animals, people, and objects look like their surroundings

conservation (kon-sur-VAY-shuhn)—the protection of animals and plants, as well as the wise use of what we get from nature

decoy (DEE-koi)—a fake animal used in hunting

dress (DRES)—to remove the organs of an animal

ecosystem (EE-koh-sis-tuhm)—a group of animals and plants that work together with their surroundings

extinction (ik-STINGK-shun)—coming to an end or dying out

range (RAYNJ)—the longest distance at which a weapon can still hit its target

scope (skohp)—a tool used for looking at objects closer

species (SPEE-sheez)—a class of living things that are the same kind

READ MORE

Carpenter, Tom. *Deer Hunting*. Lake Elmo, MN: Focus Readers, 2018.

Moran, Shelby. *We're Going Deer Hunting*. New York: PowerKids Press, 2017.

Omoth, Tyler. *Bowhunting*. Lake Elmo, MN: Focus Readers, 2018.

INTERNET SITES

White-Tailed Deer
myodfw.com/big-game-hunting/species/white-tailed-deer

Learn to Hunt Deer in 2020
dnr.state.mn.us/gohunting/learn-deer-hunt-program.html

Conservation Kids
fws.gov/international/education-zone/conservation-kids.html

INDEX